MAKING MAD MACHINES

Design   David West
                Children's Book Design
Designer   Keith Newell
Editor   Michael Flaherty
Photography Roger Vlitos

© Aladdin Books 1992

First published in
the United States in 1992 by
Gloucester Press Inc
95 Madison Ave
New York, NY 10016

Library of Congress Cataloging-in-Publication Data

Green, Jen M.
    Making mad machines / by Jen Green
        p. cm. — (Why throw it away?)
    Includes index.
    Summary: Presents step-by-step
instructions for making models of planes,
cars, and other machines using wire,
rubber bands, and other household items.
    ISBN 0-531-17326-7
    1. Machinery—Models—Juvenile
literature. [1. Machinery—Models. 2.
Models and modelmaking. 3. Handicraft.]
I. Title. II. Series.
TJ147.R58 1992
621.8—dc20   91-33867   CIP   AC

Printed in Belgium

Why throw it away?

MAKING MAD MACHINES

JEN GREEN

GLOUCESTER PRESS
New York: London: Toronto: Sydney

CONTENTS

INTRODUCTION

This book will show you how to create your own collection of mad machines – action models that move, float, race, or fly. Each of the projects is explained in easy stages. There are also more ideas about how you can adapt the models, bringing in your own imagination.

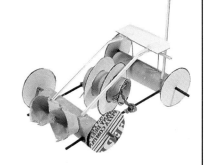

Anything goes
All the models shown here can be made with everyday junk that you and your family usually throw away. Each project includes a list of junk items that can be used to make the model. But if you haven't got one of the items suggested, don't worry; something else may do just as well.

Your junk box
Start your own collection of junk materials now. Save any materials that might come in useful, and ask your family to pass on junk to you rather than throw it away. Make sure your materials are clean before you store them in plastic bags or in a big cardboard box. For more ideas about collecting junk, see page 29. You will also find patterns and practical hints at the end of the book.

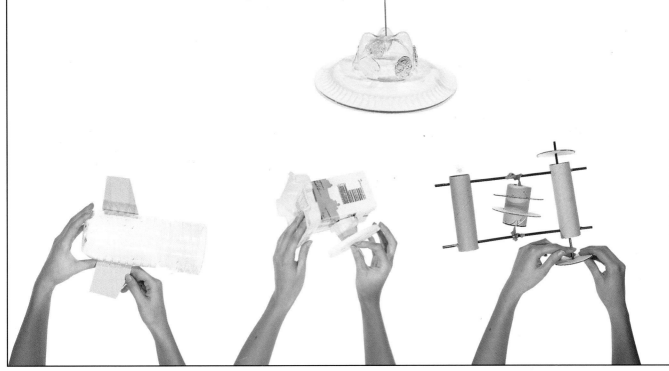

POWERED SPEEDBOAT

This simply-made speedboat with its racing crew will make waves in a pond or swimming pool, or even in the bath! Powered by a balloon, the boat will streak across the water as if jet-propelled.

STEP BY STEP

1 Using a pair of scissors, cut a clean plastic bottle in half lengthwise.
2 Pierce the back of the boat with scissors. Enlarge the hole to fit the neck of a balloon. To make the boat watertight at the front, cut a triangular-shaped wedge of plastic from the part of the bottle you have discarded. Crease it down the middle and attach it to the neck of the bottle with tape, to act as a prow.
3 Push the neck of the balloon through the hole you have made in the rear of the boat. You will need to weight the boat to prevent it from capsizing. Line the front of the boat with a lump of modeling clay, and make clay passengers. Place them in the prow (front) of the boat too, to provide more stability.

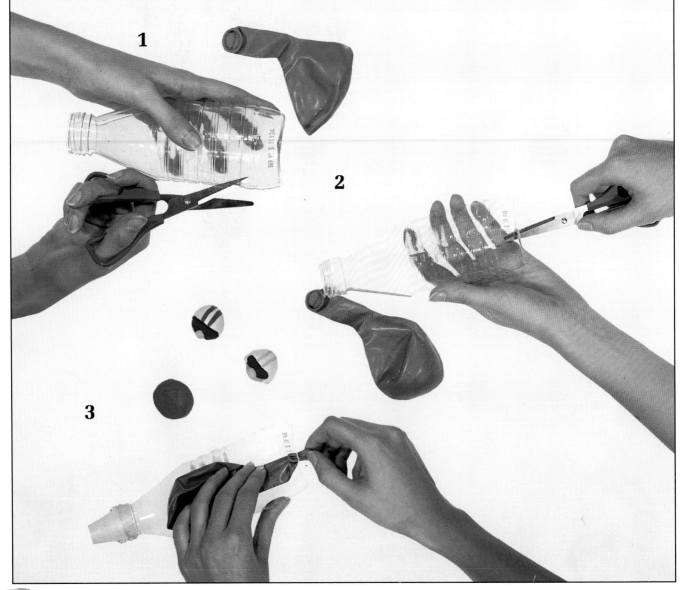

plastic bottle

balloon

scissors

modeling clay

Your modeling clay sailors could be speedboat champions, as shown here. Or you could make the crew of a fishing boat, dressed in yellow raincoats, with their catch.

To test out your speedboat, blow up the balloon. Hold the neck of the balloon tightly between your fingers to prevent air from escaping. Place the boat gently on the water and let the balloon go!

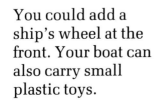

You could add a ship's wheel at the front. Your boat can also carry small plastic toys.

VIKING LONGBOAT

Viking warriors sailed the seas in the 9th and 10th centuries, on raiding missions around the coasts of Europe. Their ships had carved figureheads of monsters or serpents. This longboat design can be adapted to make a pirate ship.

STEP BY STEP

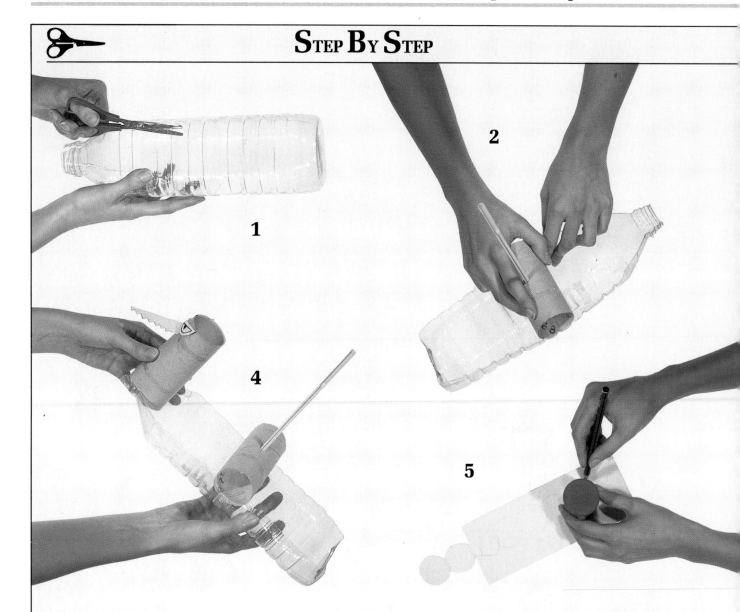

1 To make the longboat, cut a plastic bottle in half lengthwise with scissors.
2 Make a hole in a toilet paper tube. Push a straw into the hole for the mast. Wedge the tube sideways into the boat. Trim the tube if it doesn't fit.
3 Viking ships had fierce figureheads. Yours will be made with a second cardboard tube. Cut a pointed beak for it from cardboard or from the inside of an egg carton. Cut fierce-looking teeth into the beak, and glue or tape it to the tube.
4 Draw scowling eyes with a felt-tip pen. Cut them out and glue or tape them on too. Wedge the figurehead in the front of the boat.
5 Draw around a small bottle to create two rows of linked circles. Cut them out and stick them to the sides of your longboat to form two lines of Viking shields.
6 Make a sail with a square of paper or thin cardboard. Cut small slits near the top

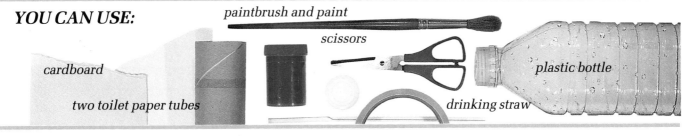

paintbrush and paint

scissors

cardboard

plastic bottle

two toilet paper tubes

drinking straw

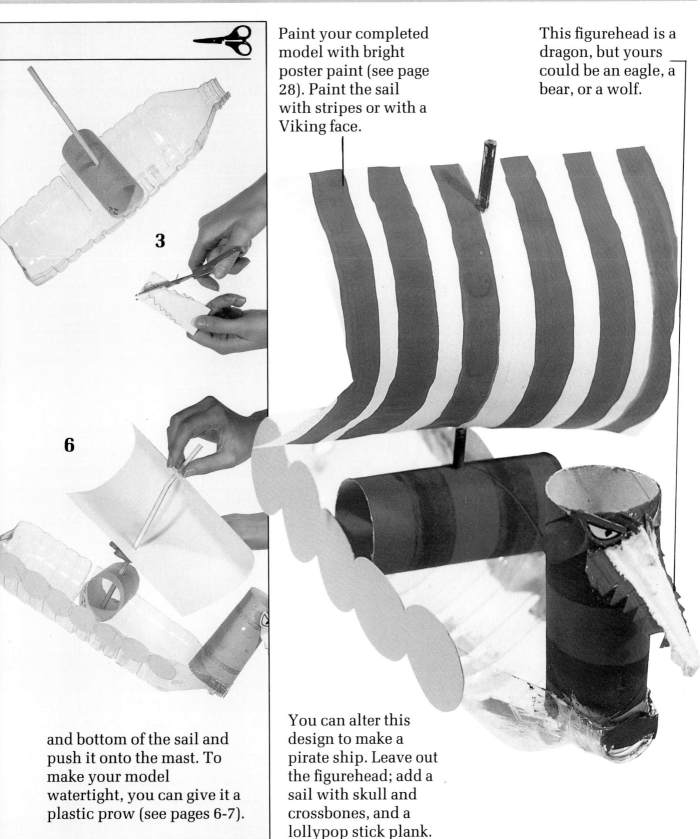

3

6

Paint your completed model with bright poster paint (see page 28). Paint the sail with stripes or with a Viking face.

This figurehead is a dragon, but yours could be an eagle, a bear, or a wolf.

and bottom of the sail and push it onto the mast. To make your model watertight, you can give it a plastic prow (see pages 6-7).

You can alter this design to make a pirate ship. Leave out the figurehead; add a sail with skull and crossbones, and a lollypop stick plank.

SPACE ROCKET

This spaceship has three stages that fit together and will be detached during a space flight. The third stage, jettisoned after launch, and the command module have rocket boosters for powering the craft on space missions.

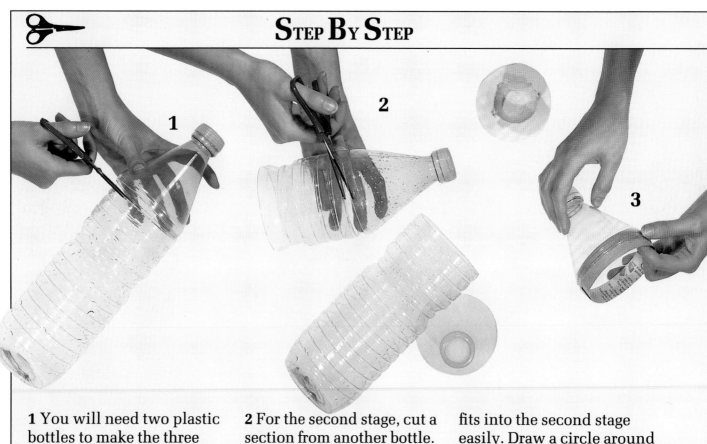

STEP BY STEP

1 You will need two plastic bottles to make the three stages of the rocket. Cut the first bottle as shown for the command module and the third stage.

2 For the second stage, cut a section from another bottle.
3 Cut a strip of cardboard and fit it inside the module to make a lip for the command module, so that it

fits into the second stage easily. Draw a circle around the bottom of the module on cardboard, and cut it out. Cut a segment from an egg carton to make a rocket

Color the rocket with thick poster paint. You could decorate it with silver foil. You could make it a ship from your country on earth – or a rocket from another planet. You could paint a window in the command module, with astronauts looking out of it.

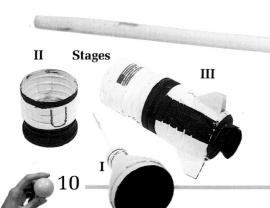

II   **Stages**

III

I

10

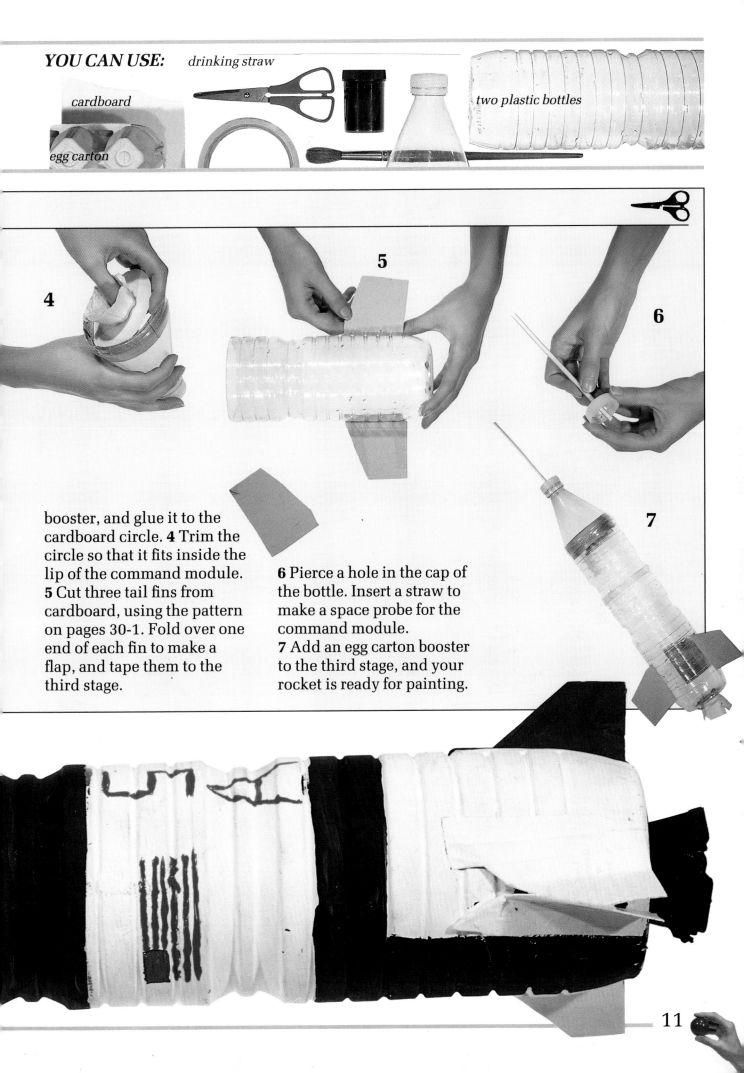

4

5

6

7

booster, and glue it to the cardboard circle. **4** Trim the circle so that it fits inside the lip of the command module. **5** Cut three tail fins from cardboard, using the pattern on pages 30-1. Fold over one end of each fin to make a flap, and tape them to the third stage.

6 Pierce a hole in the cap of the bottle. Insert a straw to make a space probe for the command module.
7 Add an egg carton booster to the third stage, and your rocket is ready for painting.

TWO-WAY TELEPHONE

These colorful telephones are easy to make and great fun to operate. When the line is pulled taut you will be able to hear a friend's voice and speak to him or her in the next room – or as far away as your string will stretch!

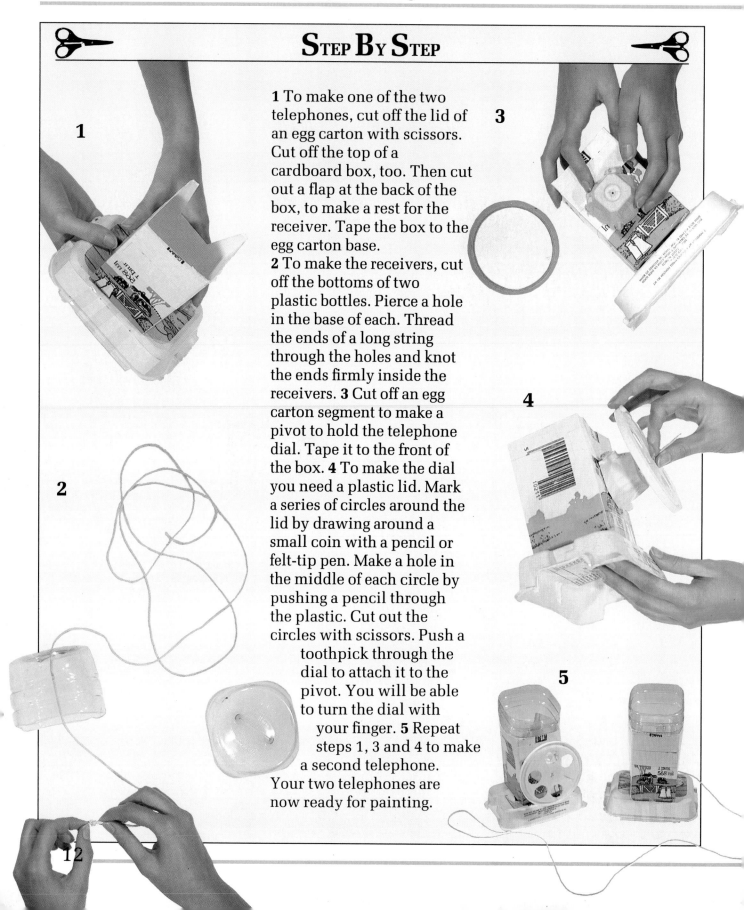

STEP BY STEP

1 To make one of the two telephones, cut off the lid of an egg carton with scissors. Cut off the top of a cardboard box, too. Then cut out a flap at the back of the box, to make a rest for the receiver. Tape the box to the egg carton base.
2 To make the receivers, cut off the bottoms of two plastic bottles. Pierce a hole in the base of each. Thread the ends of a long string through the holes and knot the ends firmly inside the receivers. **3** Cut off an egg carton segment to make a pivot to hold the telephone dial. Tape it to the front of the box. **4** To make the dial you need a plastic lid. Mark a series of circles around the lid by drawing around a small coin with a pencil or felt-tip pen. Make a hole in the middle of each circle by pushing a pencil through the plastic. Cut out the circles with scissors. Push a toothpick through the dial to attach it to the pivot. You will be able to turn the dial with your finger. **5** Repeat steps 1, 3 and 4 to make a second telephone. Your two telephones are now ready for painting.

two plastic
bottles

two
plastic
lids

string

two cardboard
boxes

two
egg cartons

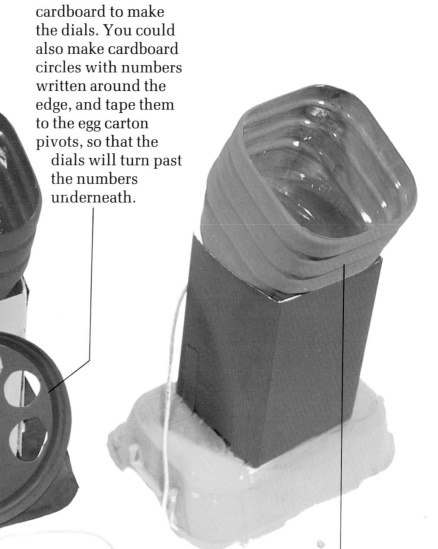

You could use cardboard to make the dials. You could also make cardboard circles with numbers written around the edge, and tape them to the egg carton pivots, so that the dials will turn past the numbers underneath.

You could also make the receivers from plastic cups.

To operate the telephones, stretch the cord tight and speak into the receiver while your friend has their ear to the other receiver.

Paint the telephone sets with bright poster paint. You could paint the working parts in different colors, as shown here.

13

INSTANT CAMERA

This trick camera contains an "instant photo" which you can use to surprise your friends. Pretend to take their picture, wait a moment to give the picture time to "develop," then produce the photo from your camera with a flourish!

1 In order to make the camera body, cut off the lids of two egg cartons and tape them together.
2 To make dials, pierce the middles of two plastic bottle tops. Use toothpicks to pin them to the top and side of the camera body. Glue or tape a large plastic cup to the front for the lens.
3 Make a viewfinder by cutting a section from a cardboard tube as shown. Fold the sides to make two flaps. Make a small square hole in the middle.

4 Glue the flaps to the camera body.
5 Make the backing for your "instant photo" by cutting a cardboard square, leaving one longer edge.
6 Find a photo you like in a magazine. Place the backing cardboard over it and trace around it with a pencil. Cut

YOU CAN USE:

- two egg carton lids
- two plastic bottle tops

magazine

cardboard

plastic cup

4

7

Attach the lens with a toothpick if you would like it to turn, as the other dials do.

You could add a strap made of ribbon, yarn, or string. Tape the strap to the camera so that you can wear the camera around your neck.

it out and glue it to the cardboard. **7** Cut a slot in the top of the camera wide enough to take the "photo," but not the long edge. Slot the photo into the camera, leaving the long edge showing. You are ready to "take a photo," and then produce your snapshot as if by magic.

You could make a series of "snapshots," with pictures from magazines, or with real photographs of your family or friends glued on. Pretend to photograph them and then produce the right – or the wrong – snapshot from your camera.

FLYING SAUCER WITH LAUNCHPAD

Do you believe that flying saucers have ever visited Earth? Many people do. This model, made with paper plates, works like a frisbee, and a flick of your wrist will send it skimming into space.

1 Make the saucer by taping together two paper plates. Cut off the bottom of a plastic bottle. 2 Make a series of circles by drawing around a circular object on cardboard. Cut out and cover the circles with silver foil. 3 Tape the bottom of the plastic bottle to your saucer, to make a viewing deck. (You could paint the plate inside the viewing deck before you tape it down securely). Tape the foil circles around the viewing deck. 4 To make the launch pad, cut off the bottom of another plastic bottle. Pierce three holes evenly spaced around the rim. Push straws through the holes to make the legs. Tape the straws inside the rim. 5 Push a toothpick into the top of the viewing deck of the flying machine to make an aerial.

YOU CAN USE:
cardboard
straws   silver foil
two plastic bottles
toothpick
two paper plates

What kind of life-forms travel in your flying saucer? You could cut out the shapes of aliens or astronauts, and tape them inside the viewing deck.

You could decorate the saucer with buttons or with ring-pulls from soft beverage cans. In between missions, your flying saucer rests on its launch pad for repairs or refueling.

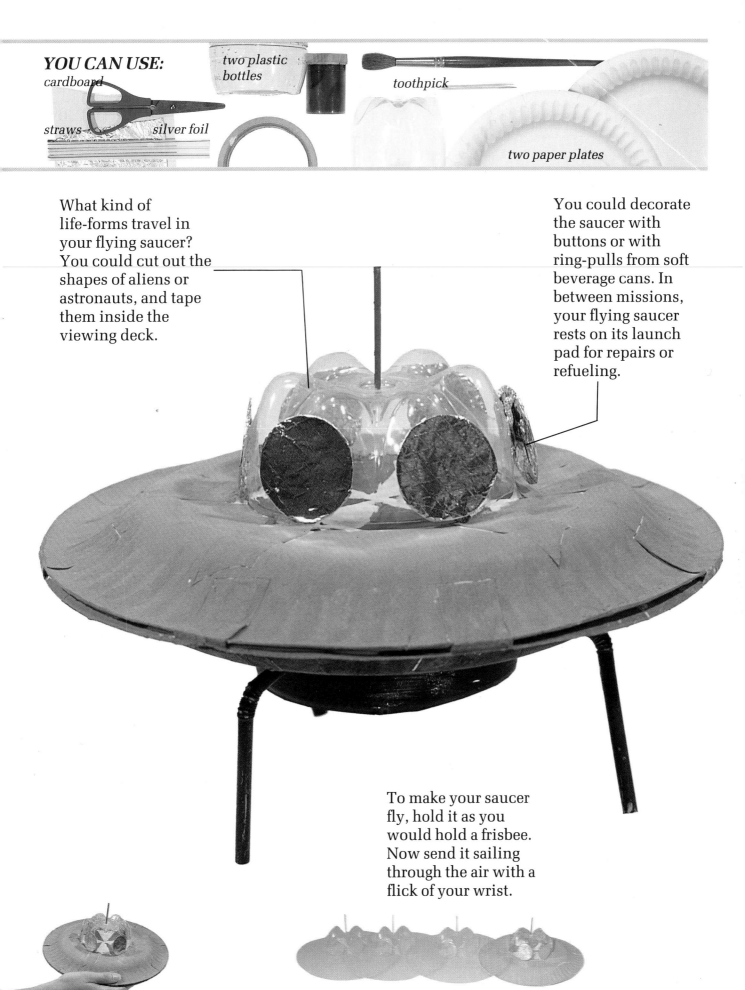

To make your saucer fly, hold it as you would hold a frisbee. Now send it sailing through the air with a flick of your wrist.

17

TELEVISION

This television is fitted with a scroll that you can turn to make images move across the screen. Cut out the pictures you want to appear on screen and put on a show to impress your family and friends.

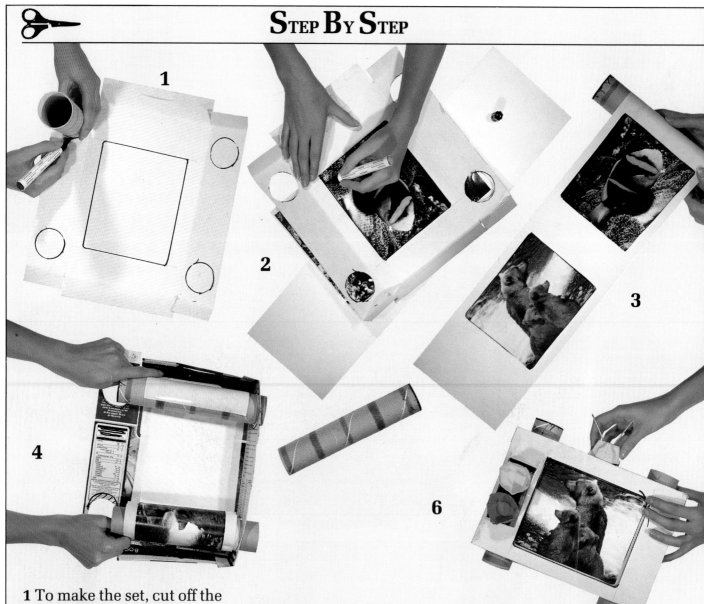

1 To make the set, cut off the back of a cardboard box, leaving the front, top, bottom, and sides. Mark a distance of 1 in from both ends of each side. You will need two paper towel tubes to make the scroll. Put the edge of one of the tubes where you've marked. Trace around it with a felt-tip pen. Pierce the center of the circles and cut them out.

2 Choose pictures you want to appear on screen from comics or magazines. Cut them out. Mark a screen to fit your pictures on the front of the box, and cut it out.

3 To make the scroll, you need a long strip of paper that just fits inside your television. Glue the pictures along the strip. When the glue is dry, roll the strip around the cardboard tubes. Secure the ends to the rolls with tape.

4 Fit the scroll inside the television, pushing the ends of the tubes through the holes in the box.

5 Secure the ends outside the box with toothpicks.

two egg cartons

cardboard box

paper towel tubes

5

6 To finish the television, make an aerial by pushing toothpicks into the segment of an egg carton. Make dials from two more segments. Glue them onto round cardboard bases. Tape the aerial and dials onto the set.

Twist the tube to make your pictures move across the screen.

DRAG RACER

Drag racers or dragsters are cars with very powerful engines that are built to travel as fast as possible. With its streamlined body and impressive exhaust system, your dragster will be ready to win any race.

STEP BY STEP

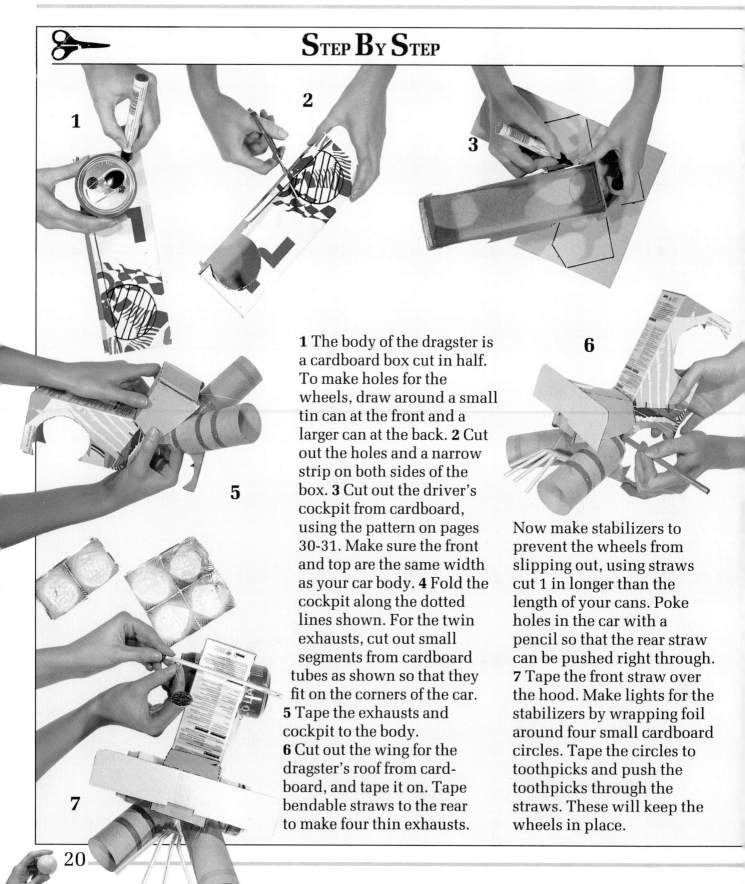

1 The body of the dragster is a cardboard box cut in half. To make holes for the wheels, draw around a small tin can at the front and a larger can at the back. 2 Cut out the holes and a narrow strip on both sides of the box. 3 Cut out the driver's cockpit from cardboard, using the pattern on pages 30-31. Make sure the front and top are the same width as your car body. 4 Fold the cockpit along the dotted lines shown. For the twin exhausts, cut out small segments from cardboard tubes as shown so that they fit on the corners of the car. 5 Tape the exhausts and cockpit to the body.
6 Cut out the wing for the dragster's roof from cardboard, and tape it on. Tape bendable straws to the rear to make four thin exhausts.

Now make stabilizers to prevent the wheels from slipping out, using straws cut 1 in longer than the length of your cans. Poke holes in the car with a pencil so that the rear straw can be pushed right through. 7 Tape the front straw over the hood. Make lights for the stabilizers by wrapping foil around four small cardboard circles. Tape the circles to toothpicks and push the toothpicks through the straws. These will keep the wheels in place.

cardboard
box

toothpicks

two cardboard tubes

straws

foil

candy
box tray

two
beverage
cans

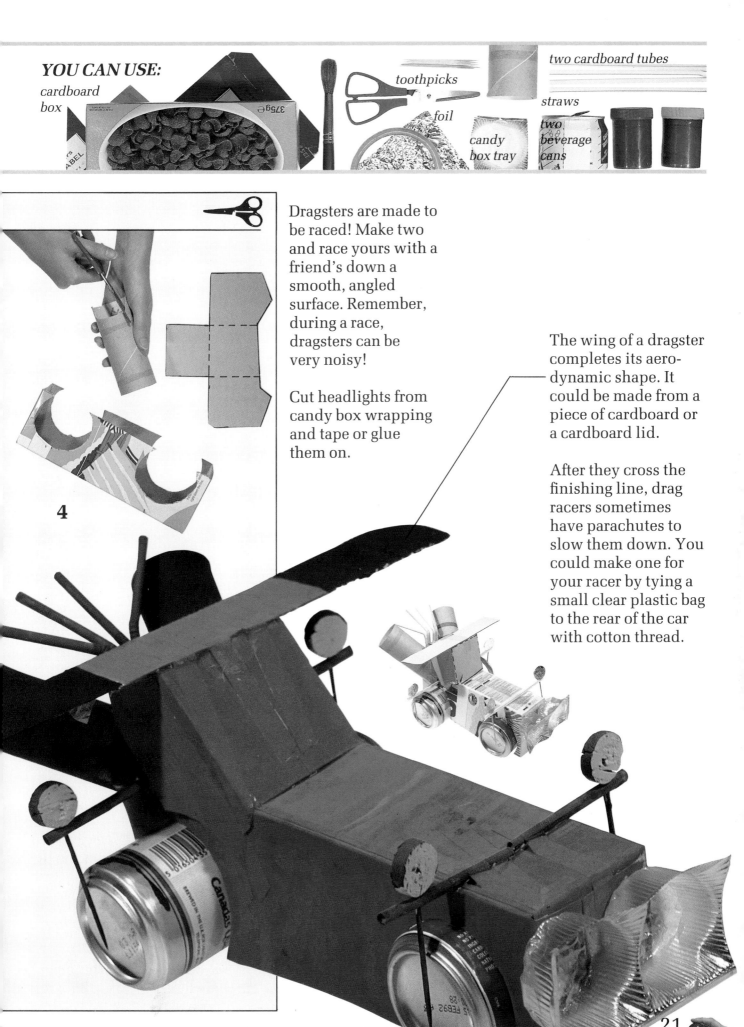

Dragsters are made to be raced! Make two and race yours with a friend's down a smooth, angled surface. Remember, during a race, dragsters can be very noisy!

Cut headlights from candy box wrapping and tape or glue them on.

The wing of a dragster completes its aero-dynamic shape. It could be made from a piece of cardboard or a cardboard lid.

After they cross the finishing line, drag racers sometimes have parachutes to slow them down. You could make one for your racer by tying a small clear plastic bag to the rear of the car with cotton thread.

4

BIPLANE WITH FLYING ACE

Biplanes were used by the British, French, and German forces during World War I. With a fearless pilot in the cockpit, this model has a double wing and a propeller that turns as the plane flies through the air.

STEP BY STEP

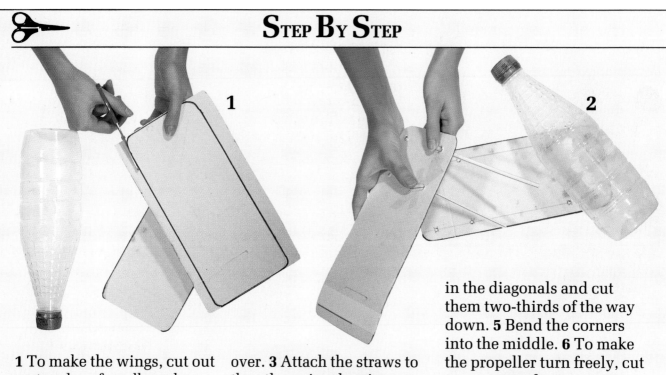

1 To make the wings, cut out rectangles of cardboard, using the pattern on pages 30-31. Make sure the bottle that forms your plane's body fits between the two middle crosses shown on the pattern. Make holes on the crosses. **2** Push drinking straws through the holes in one wing, and bend the ends over. **3** Attach the straws to the other wing, leaving a gap that fits your bottle between the wings. Tape the bottle in place. Cut out cardboard shapes for the tail fin as shown. Fold the top fin and tape it to the crossfin. Tape the fin to the back of the plane. **4** Make the propeller with a square of paper. Mark in the diagonals and cut them two-thirds of the way down. **5** Bend the corners into the middle. **6** To make the propeller turn freely, cut two squares from a straw. Thread one square onto a pin, pin the corners of the propeller to its center, and thread on the other square. **7** Pierce a hole in the bottle top. Put clay inside the top to weight down the plane's nose. Pin the propeller onto the plane.

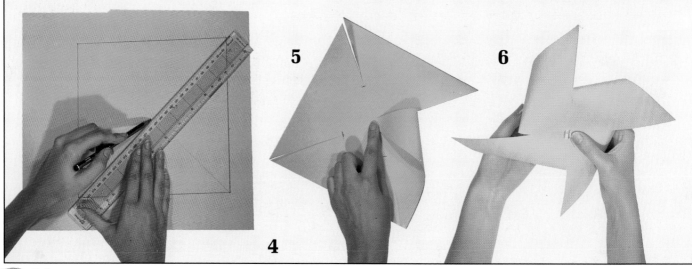

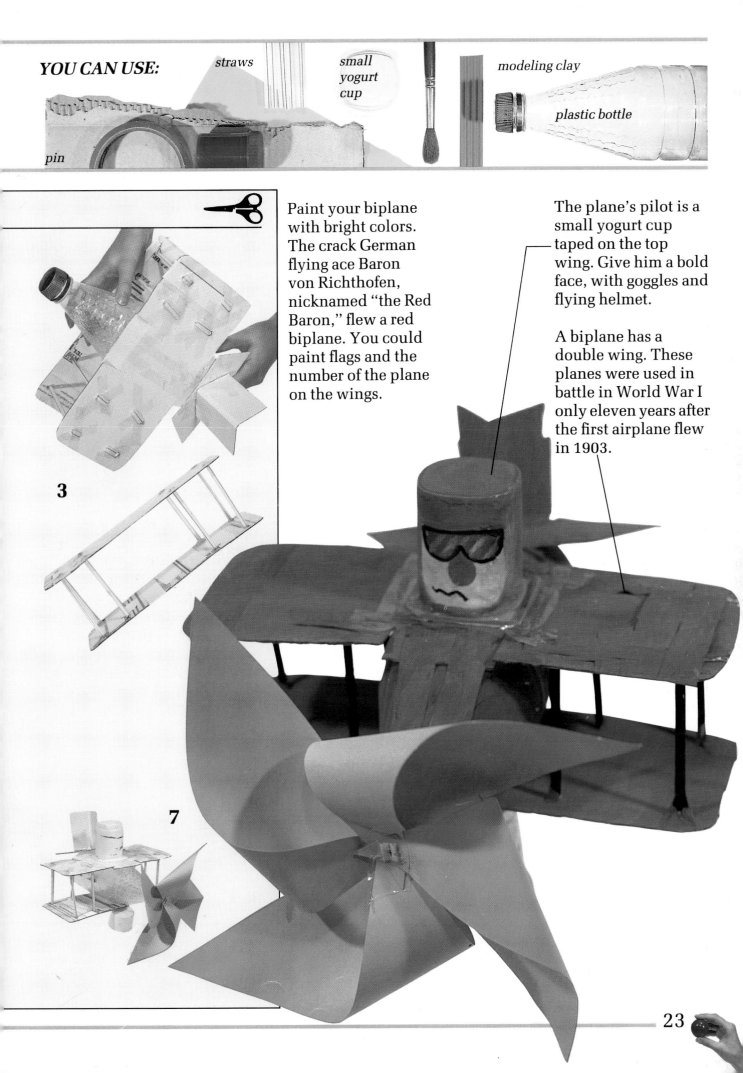

straws

small
yogurt
cup

modeling clay

plastic bottle

pin

3

Paint your biplane with bright colors. The crack German flying ace Baron von Richthofen, nicknamed "the Red Baron," flew a red biplane. You could paint flags and the number of the plane on the wings.

The plane's pilot is a small yogurt cup taped on the top wing. Give him a bold face, with goggles and flying helmet.

A biplane has a double wing. These planes were used in battle in World War I only eleven years after the first airplane flew in 1903.

7

FLYING THE BIPLANE

Your biplane flies from strings attached to a garden stick control frame. As the plane flies, the propeller spins around. The frame can be held in various positions to make the plane perform different maneuvers.

STEP BY STEP

1 To make the control frame, you will need a piece of garden stick. Use scissors to make notches in the stick about 0.5 in from each end. Cut two pieces of string about 2 feet long. Tie one end of each piece around the notches in the stick.
2 Attach the other ends of the strings securely to the

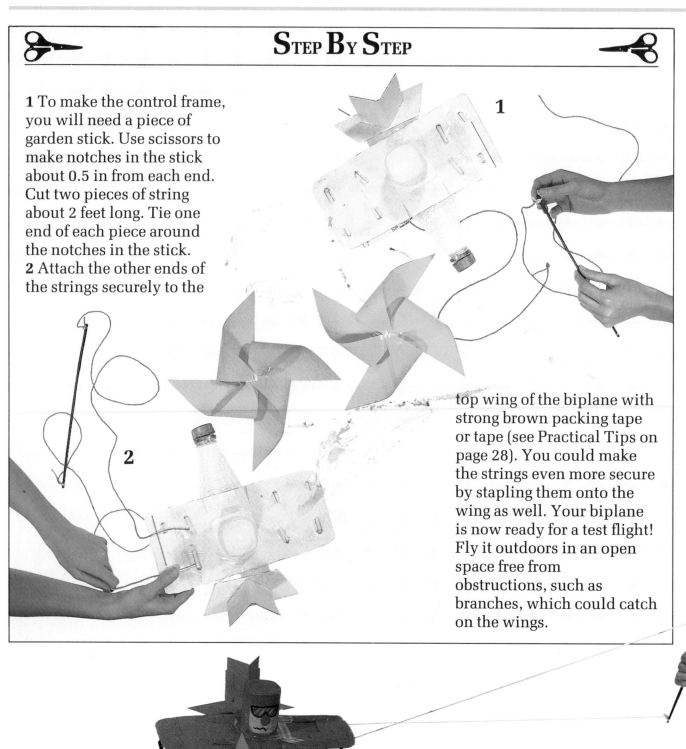

top wing of the biplane with strong brown packing tape or tape (see Practical Tips on page 28). You could make the strings even more secure by stapling them onto the wing as well. Your biplane is now ready for a test flight! Fly it outdoors in an open space free from obstructions, such as branches, which could catch on the wings.

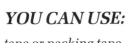

Hold the stick frame with your arm outstretched and the plane dangling down. Swing around in a circle and watch the plane as it lifts off into the air.

The flight of the biplane can be controlled by the angle at which you hold the frame. Twist your wrist to make the plane swoop and dive.

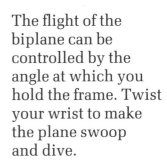

Twist your wrist up to make the biplane ascend. Twist it down to make the plane spiral downward.

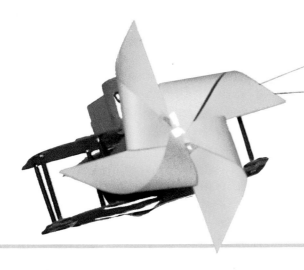

You could also try standing still and whirling the plane above your head like a lasso.

Moon Buggy

This curious vehicle has a powerful dynamo driven by rubber bands. It is designed to carry small extraterrestrials over moon terrain – and over any smooth surface in your home!

Step By Step

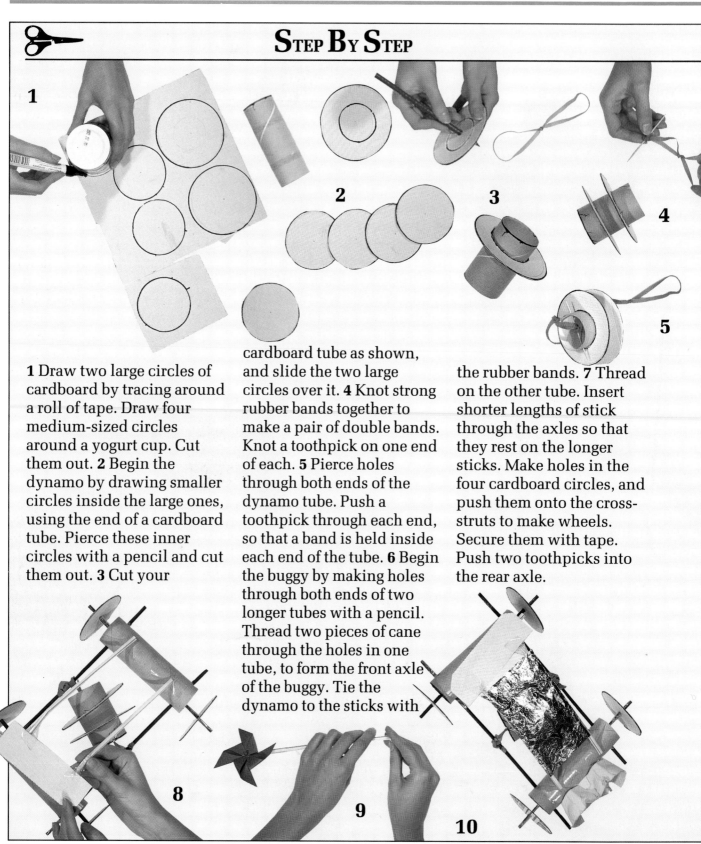

1 Draw two large circles of cardboard by tracing around a roll of tape. Draw four medium-sized circles around a yogurt cup. Cut them out. **2** Begin the dynamo by drawing smaller circles inside the large ones, using the end of a cardboard tube. Pierce these inner circles with a pencil and cut them out. **3** Cut your cardboard tube as shown, and slide the two large circles over it. **4** Knot strong rubber bands together to make a pair of double bands. Knot a toothpick on one end of each. **5** Pierce holes through both ends of the dynamo tube. Push a toothpick through each end, so that a band is held inside each end of the tube. **6** Begin the buggy by making holes through both ends of two longer tubes with a pencil. Thread two pieces of cane through the holes in one tube, to form the front axle of the buggy. Tie the dynamo to the sticks with the rubber bands. **7** Thread on the other tube. Insert shorter lengths of stick through the axles so that they rest on the longer sticks. Make holes in the four cardboard circles, and push them onto the cross-struts to make wheels. Secure them with tape. Push two toothpicks into the rear axle.

YOU CAN USE:

foil

egg carton

cardboard toothpicks

four pieces of garden-stick

stout cardboard tube

6

7

To finish the buggy:
8 Push a straw cross-strut onto the toothpick. Then push the ends of two long straws on. Add a rectangle of cardboard for a seat. Tape the other ends of the long straws to the front axle. **9** Make a small paper wind-mill (see pages 22-23). Pin it to a straw and tape the straw to the rear axle. Wrap a piece of foil around the straws. Tape on headlights cut from an egg carton.

PRACTICAL TIPS

Below are a few practical hints that will help you with some of the projects described in this book.

FASTENING
Use this tip for making the biplane (pp 24-25) and whenever you need to fasten string securely.

To fasten thread or string to cardboard, tie a double knot at one end. Place the knot on the cardboard. Lay strips of tape in front of the knot, and press down firmly.

To make your fastening even more secure, you could use packing tape. If you have a stapler, you could staple the knot in place before you tape it down.

SCORING
Scoring is a way of producing a neat and accurate fold in a piece of paper. You can use this technique to make the rocket's fin, and in other projects, too.

To score paper, place your ruler along the line you want to fold. Press the edge of your scissors lightly along the paper, using the ruler as a guide. Don't press too hard or you may cut through the paper! Then fold along the line you have scored.

PAINTING
It may be difficult to get paint to stick to tape, and to plastic surfaces. If so, this tip will help.

Poster paint has been used to decorate many of the projects in this book. It is usually diluted with water. This paint will stick to plastic if you squirt a little dishwashing liquid into your mixing water. Mix it well before you begin.

RUBBER: rubber bands, balls, balloons, old rubber gloves.

MORE JUNK IDEAS

NATURAL MATERIALS: twigs, leaves, petals, acorns, chestnuts, nuts, pinecones, bark, shells, pebbles, sponge, cork, feathers.

The materials used most often in this book have been paper, cardboard and plastic packaging. Below are some more suggestions about the kinds of junk that can be used to make and decorate your models.

PAPER: newspapers, comics and magazines, postcards and birthday cards, unused wallpaper, tissue.

WOOD: spent matches, garden sticks, cotton spools, lollypop sticks.

PLASTIC: food containers, candy and snack wrappers, buttons, broken toys.

FABRIC: yarn, socks, old clothes or sheets, cloth and felt scraps.

METAL: soft beverage cans, foil, springs, pipe cleaners, hangers, paper clips.

PATTERNS

To use these patterns:
1 Trace the pattern shape onto tracing paper.
2 Turn the tracing over, and place it on top of the paper or cardboard on which you want the image to appear. Scribble over the lines showing through the paper with your pencil. A mirror image of the pattern will appear on the cardboard.

▷ Trace this pattern to make the rocket's fin (see pages 10-11)

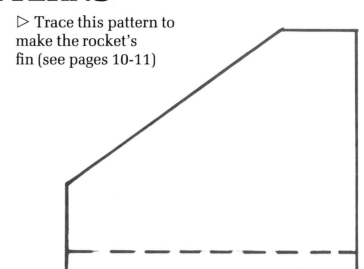

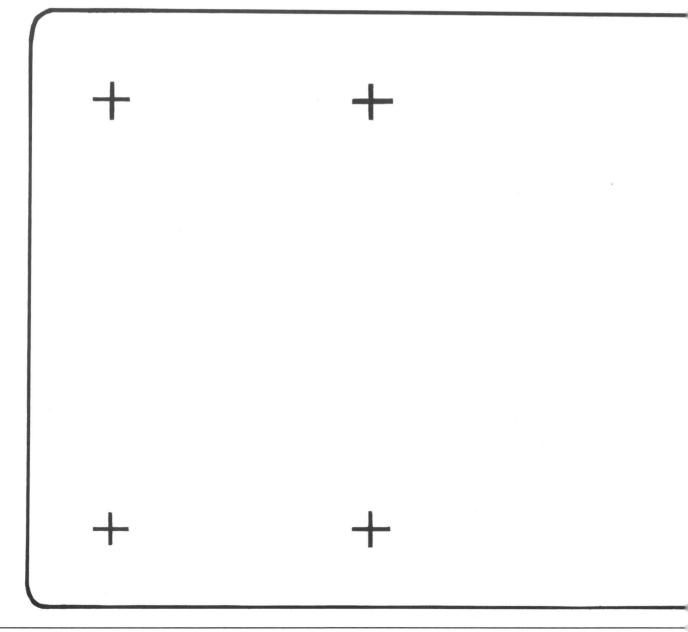

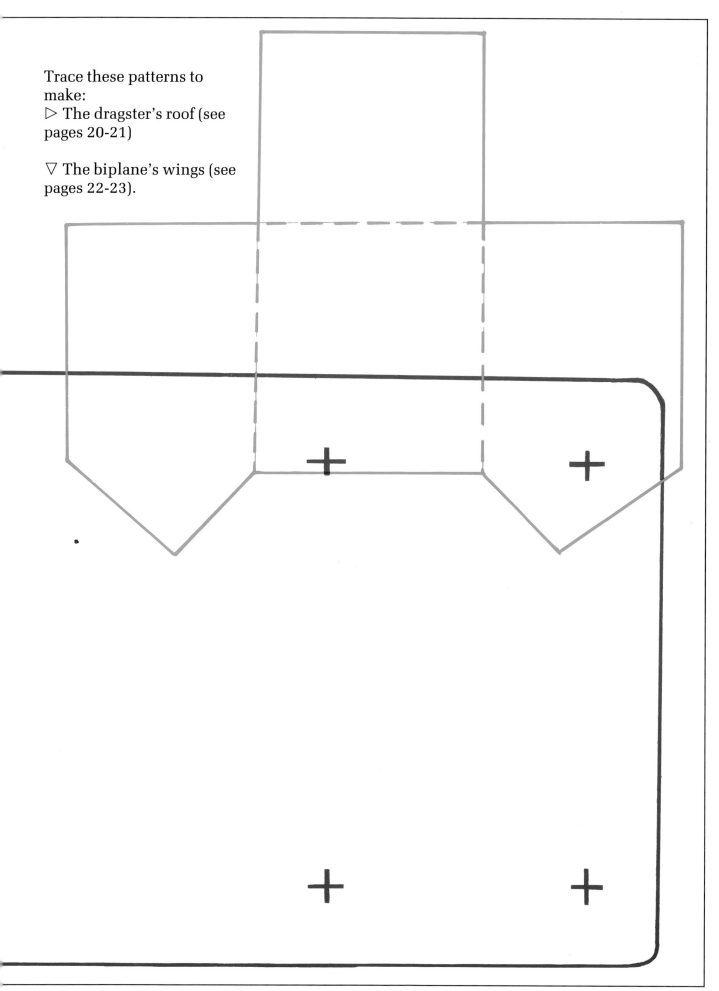

Trace these patterns to make:
▷ The dragster's roof (see pages 20-21)

▽ The biplane's wings (see pages 22-23).

INDEX

PRINTED IN BELGIUM BY
proost
INTERNATIONAL BOOK PRODUCTION